K M A Ahamed Zubair

Four Great Scholars of Tamil Nadu

AF612763

K M A Ahamed Zubair

Four Great Scholars of Tamil Nadu

Falah Wali | Moulana Baqir Agah | Moulana Abdul Ali Bahrul Uloom |Sharaful Mulk Bahadur

Noor Publishing

Imprint
Any brand names and product names mentioned in this book are subject to trademark, brand or patent protection and are trademarks or registered trademarks of their respective holders. The use of brand names, product names, common names, trade names, product descriptions etc. even without a particular marking in this work is in no way to be construed to mean that such names may be regarded as unrestricted in respect of trademark and brand protection legislation and could thus be used by anyone.

Cover image: www.ingimage.com

Publisher:
Noor Publishing
is a trademark of
Dodo Books Indian Ocean Ltd. and OmniScriptum S.R.L publishing group

120 High Road, East Finchley, London, N2 9ED, United Kingdom
Str. Armeneasca 28/1, office 1, Chisinau MD-2012, Republic of Moldova, Europe
Printed at: see last page
ISBN: 978-620-7-47923-8

Copyright © K M A Ahamed Zubair
Copyright © 2024 Dodo Books Indian Ocean Ltd. and OmniScriptum S.R.L publishing group

Four Great Scholars of Tamil Nadu

Falah Wali | Moulana Baqir Agah | Moulana Abdul Ali Bahrul Uloom | Sharaful Mulk Bahadur

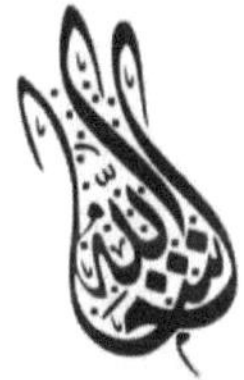

Dr.K.M.A.Ahamed Zubair

Associate Professor of Arabic, The New College, Chennai 600 014, India

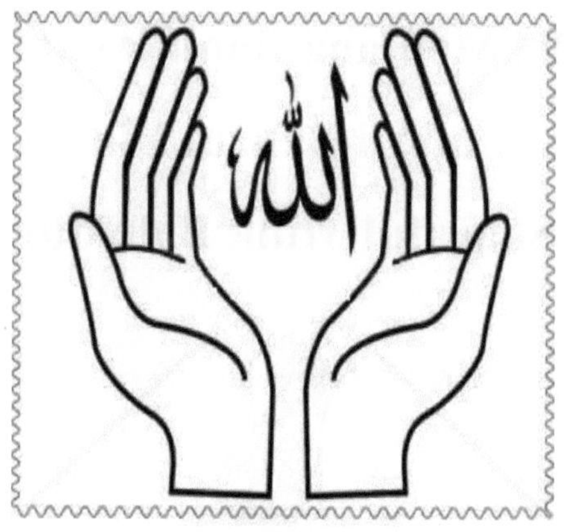

اللغة العربية تحمل كلمة الله، وروح محمد ﷺ، وسر الإسلام،

This work has been dedicated to the Indian Islamic Missionaries

(1500-1800)

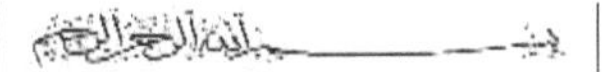

Preface

Four Great Scholars of Tamil Nadu

In the annals of intellectual history, the names of Moulana Baqir Agah, Moulana Abdul Ali Bahrul Uloom, and Sharaful Mulk Bahadur stand as towering figures, each contributing significantly to their respective fields of Islamic scholarship. As we embark on a journey through the corridors of their scholarly legacies, we are reminded of the enduring power of knowledge to illuminate the darkest recesses of ignorance and superstition.

The compendium presented here serves as a testament to the enduring relevance of their teachings, offering readers a glimpse into the depth and breadth of their intellectual prowess. From theological treatises and philosophical inquiries to critical analyses and explorations of mysticism, each chapter encapsulates the profound insights and unwavering dedication to truth that characterized these scholars.

Through meticulous scholarship and a relentless pursuit of understanding, they forged paths towards enlightenment, leaving indelible marks on the landscape of Islamic thought. Rooted in rich traditions and engaged with the philosophical currents of their eras, their works continue to inspire seekers of truth and knowledge across generations.

As we delve into the pages of this compendium, let us approach each chapter with humility and an open mind, recognizing the wisdom of generations past waiting to be unearthed and embraced by all who seek enlightenment.

Dr K M A Ahamed Zubair

Contents

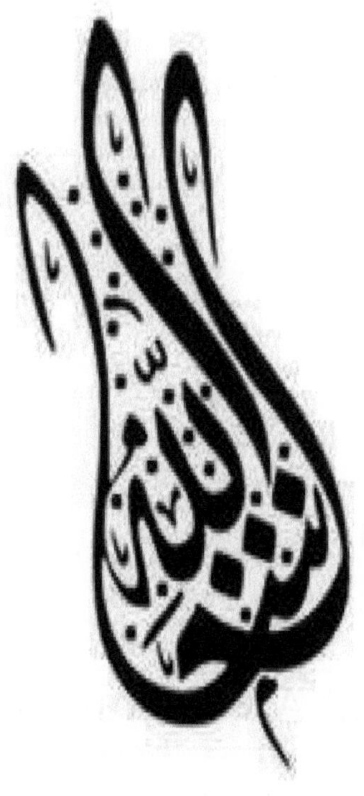

1. **Sheikh Habib Muhammad Sadaqathullah, known as Falah Wali (or) Fallak Thambi Wali** (1268 - 1360 AH / 1851 - 1941 CE)

Muhammad Sadaqathullah, also known as Sheikh Habib Muhammad, the son of Noah Sahib, known as Noor Sahib, the son of Sayyid Muhammad Ismail, the son of Sadaqathullah, the son of "Mina" Ahmad, the son of Mahmood, the son of Sadaq Ibrahim Marikar, the son of Alauddin, the son of Sheikh Ali "al-Nuski," known as the “Milk Drinker”, buried in the Mosque of Al-Makhdum in Kayalpattanam. He is Sheikh Ali al-Nuski, the son of the scholar Ahmad, the son of Sheikh Muhammad, the son of Sheikh Ahmad, the son of Sheikh Shihabuddin, the son of Sheikh Muhammad Khidr, the son of Sheikh Muhammad Khalji, the son of Sheikh Hassan, the son of Sheikh Abdul Aziz, the son of Sheikh Hashim, the son of Sheikh Abd Manaf, the son of Sheikh Qusay, the son of Sheikh Kilab, the son of Sheikh Murrah, the son of Sheikh Ritam, the son of Sheikh Abdul Rahman, the son of the revered Abu Bakr al-Siddiq, may Allah be pleased with him.

The father of Sheikh Falah Thambi is the brother Muhammad, known as "Lebbai Sahib," and the grandfather of Sheikh Falah Thambi, known as "Hazrat Alam Sahib," is buried in the Qadiriyya seminary courtyard in the town of Kayalpattanam . The father of Sheikh Falah Thambi, Noor Sahib, came to the city of Kilakkarai and settled there.

He married Muhammad Fatima, the daughter of Wana Sahib, the son of Habib Muhammad Marikar, known as Malik Habib (Habib Arasar).

Malik Habib, buried in the western dome of the famous "Odakkarai" mosque in Kilakkarai , was the husband of Sarah Umma and Fatima, the daughters of "Lebbai Ghani."

Sheikh Falah Muhammad was born to the aforementioned Muhammad Fatima in Kilakkarai on Monday, the 12th of Rabi' al-Awwal in the year 1268 AH. His father named him Habib Muhammad Sadaqathullah, and people used to call him by the nickname Fallak Thambi.

When he turned three years old, his father Noah Sahib passed away by the will of Allah. His mother raised him with great care, educated him with good manners, and refined him with proper training. His character was known to be truthful and reliable in his words. The people were amazed by his good manners and intelligence. When Sheikh was ten years old, he had memorized the Holy Qur'an by heart.

According to some accounts, the word "Falah" changed to "Fallak" in the Tamil language. In Tamil, the word "Fallak" referred to a "litter" in Arabic, and people used to carry Sheikh Habib Muhammad Sadaqathullah in one of these litters when he was young. Hence, people started calling him "Fallak Wali."

He learned the religious and secular sciences from the great scholar Sayyid Muhammad Alam Sahib, known as Imam Al-Aroos, in the Aroosiyya school. He studied Tafsir, Hadith, and Sufism under Imam Al-Aroos, who took him as a disciple and guide and gave him the spiritual pledge. He achieved great success through his guidance and gained much through his instruction.

His quick understanding and intelligence caught the attention of his teacher, who called him Falah Thambi. After this, he became known among the people as Falah Waliullah. He absorbed spirituality from his teacher and later became a famous Sufi known as Falah Wali. He became well-known among the people for his numerous miracles.

He was a companion to his two sons: one was Sheikh Sayyid Abdul Qadir, known as "Sahibul Khalwah," and the other was Ahmad Mustafa, known as "Sahibul Jalwah".

When he reached the age of twenty-three, he traveled with his teacher, Sheikh Imam Al-Aroos, to Mecca and Medina to perform Hajj and Umrah and to visit the tomb of the Prophet Muhammad, peace be upon him. He also visited Iraq, Damascus, Palestine, and Egypt with his teacher, where he met great scholars and visited the graves of the prophets.

When he was about twenty-four years old, he married Aisha, the daughter of Qadir Sahib bin Wappa Sahib, the son of Habib Muhammad Marikar, known as "Malik Habib." Aisha lived for only three years. He then married her sister, Muhammad Nachiyar, from whom he had a son, Muhammad Sahib, who married Khadija Umma, the daughter of Sadaqathullah. She was a servant to the esteemed Sheikh Fallak Wali.

At the age of thirty-two, he traveled to the island of Sarandib (Sri Lanka) with his friend, Sayyid Abdul Qadir, with the permission of their teacher, Imam Al-Aroos. The people of the island welcomed them joyfully, benefited from their advice, and learned from their knowledge. After returning from Sarandib with his friend to Kilakkarai , his friend isolated himself from the people and remained in seclusion for worship in the year 1300 AH.

Sheikh Falah Wali read a book called "Murshid al-Tullab," which explained aspects of Sufism. He was always fond of Sultan Sayyid Ibrahim Shaheed in Erwadi. He praised him in prose and poetry, calling him "Ya Badshah" and "Ya Sayyid Ibrahim al-Wadad." Sayyid Ibrahim came from Medina by the command of Prophet Muhammad, peace be upon him, with troops to spread Islam in Sindh in 557 AH. He arrived in southern India during the Pandya dynasty in 582 AH and established an Islamic Sultanate.

Sheikh Falah Wali was wealthy and prosperous. He taught religious sciences to students and spent his time studying at the Aroosiyya school in Kilakkarai . People gathered for his Dhikr sessions, where he recited poems with passion, praising the virtuous, saints, and nobles. He had many miracles. The famous Tamil writer, Sheikh Abdul Rahim, wrote seventeen pages about the miracles of Sheikh Habib Muhammad Fallak Thambi in his book "Tareekh al-Awliya" from pages 487 to 513 in volume four.

After sunrise and before sunset, he recited "La ilaha illallah" and sent blessings upon the Prophet Muhammad, peace be upon him, ten times, "Ya Rahman Ya Daim" twenty times, "Ya Hayy" fifteen times, and "Ya Muhyi" sixty times daily. He also recited Surah Al-Ikhlas three times.

When he turned seventy, he went to the blessed town of Thondi. The people of Thondi and Nambuthalay invited him to their town, and he traveled with them from his hometown. Sheikh, along with his loved ones, visited the tomb of Sheikh Qutb al-Zaman Abu Bakr Thondi Waliullah, who was his maternal grandfather. His mother was Fatima, the daughter of Lebbai Ghani, the son of Abu Bakr Thondi.

He composed many poems about his grandfather, Sheikh Abu Bakr Thondi, may Allah have mercy on him, and often traveled to various towns from his hometown, Kilakkarai. He wrote an eighty-four-line poem about Sheikh Abu Bakr Thondi, which begins with the following verses:

Praise be to the Merciful Lord

And the Generous, Gracious One

And prayers and exalted peace

Upon Muhammad, the guide

And satisfaction and mercy upon the qutbs

And the honorable, noble ones

He is generous and glorious

And lofty and praiseworthy

And the truth and faith endure

Throughout all time

Always obedient and active

And eloquent in speech and word

Perfected among the saints

Scholarly and virtuous

And it concludes with the following verses:

Merciful and gracious in every state and time

With great honor and dignity

And upon his family and companions with their generosity

And the great and beloved saints

Among them Sheikh Abu Bakr

The revered and exalted

Sheikh Abu Bakr the qutb

With certainty and conviction

Sheikh Abu Bakr the qutb

In intentions and actions

Sheikh Abu Bakr the qutb

With honored and pure ones

Sheikh Abu Bakr the qutb

With generosity, glory, and radiance

And broaden our life and theirs

And raise love and devotion

With Sheikh Abu Bakr the qutb

Improve our state and theirs

With good words and their words

And intentions and actions and their actions

With Sheikh Abu Bakr the qutb

The qutbs and saints

And the pious and pure

And the ascetics and virtuous

With Sheikh Abu Bakr the qutb

Merciful and unified

With the sanctity of God and uniqueness

With majesty and beauty descended

With eternal praise and gratitude

An another poem by Sheikh Fallak Wali about his grandfather Sheikh Abu Bakr Thondi contains twenty-eight verses, starting with:

Oh, the greatest of saints

With purity and virtue

You are lofty in exaltation

And adorned with glory

Wearing a robe of greatness

And a turban of honor and emblem

Oh, chief of the merciful

Oh, companion of the virtuous

Oh, remover of all distress

And veil and evil

Oh, honored and exalted

Oh, bearer of the highest

Oh, the pious and abstinent

Oh, the one who remains diligent

The merciful and beautiful

Oh, illuminating moon

With purity and radiance

Oh, discerning moon

Close to contradictions

Oh, ocean of generous bestowal

Extensive and broad

Oh, one whose heart is firm

Strengthened by the pure

Abu Bakr was a qutb

And the lofty in exaltation

Abu Bakr was a qutb

Wearing the crown of generosity

Abu Bakr was a qutb

Oh, precious among the pure

Abu Bakr was a qutb

With weight and apology

Abu Bakr was a qutb

Oh, perfected and honored

Abu Bakr was a qutb

Oh, the one who finds and honors

Abu Bakr was a qutb

He is submissive to God

Abu Bakr was a qutb

With light and radiance

Abu Bakr was a qutb

Knowledgeable and wise

Abu Bakr was a qutb

In any exhaustion and breadth

Abu Bakr was a qutb

He contains the star of knowledge and thought.

And work and remembrance

Achieving purpose and goal

Voluntarily and broadly

Protect us from poverty

And illness and hardship

Abu Bakr was a qutb

Generous in favor and grace

Abu Bakr was a qutb

Then from narrowness and insignificance

Abu Bakr was a qutb

This third poem was also recited by Sheikh Fallak Wali about his grandfather Sheikh Abu Bakr Thondi, and some verses from the poem are as follows:

Always obedient with certain knowledge

Advising with true advice and certain truth

Bringing closer with closeness

True in health and certain vision

Abu Bakr is a renowned qutb

And a drinker of the cup of love

Witnessing from the witnessed

Obligatory and voluntary beloved

Abu Bakr is a renowned qutb

One, unique, and worshipped

Abu Bakr is a renowned qutb

The Eternal, Sustainer, and intended

When he reached the age of ninety-two, he desired to move on and wept for days before his death, praying to the Merciful. Allah, the Almighty, took him in His mercy gently before the time of Friday on the twenty-fifth of Rabi' al-Akhir in the year 1360 AH. His funeral prayer was led by his successor, the learned Sheikh Sayyid Ahmad Kabir, at the "Sahil

Wadi" mosque in Kilakkarai . He was buried after Maghrib on Saturday in the garden of the new mosque in Kilakkarai .

Habib Muhammad Sadaqathullah also composed poems in the Tamil language, including a famous poem titled "Allah Munajat." People read this Munajat in India, Sarandib (Sri Lanka), Malaysia, Singapore, and various other places.

Sheikh Tayka Ahmad Nasir bin Sheikh Tayka Shuaib Alam published some of Sheikh Fallak Wali's poetry as a "Diwan" (Collection) in the year 1403 AH / 1982 CE in Mumbai.

Once, a woman came to Sheikh Habib Muhammad Sadaqathullah, known as Fallak Thambi Waliullah, and told him that her children were dying before birth. The Sheikh recited some verses from the Quran over water and asked her to drink it. The Sheikh said that she would then give birth to living children. The following year, by the grace of Allah, the woman gave birth to a healthy son and named him "Fallak Thambi."

2. Moulana Baqir Agah

In the annals of Islamic scholarship, few figures loom as large as Moulana Baqir Agah (1158-1220), whose profound contributions to theological discourse and intellectual inquiry continue to resonate across the centuries. As we embark on a journey through the corridors of his scholarly legacy, we are reminded of the enduring power of knowledge to illuminate the darkest recesses of ignorance and superstition.

This compendium stands as a testament to the enduring relevance of Moulana Baqir Agah's teachings, offering readers a glimpse into the depth and breadth of his intellectual prowess. Through meticulous scholarship and unwavering dedication to truth, he forged a path towards enlightenment, leaving an indelible mark on the landscape of Islamic thought.

Introduction:

Within the pages of this compendium, readers will find a treasure trove of theological treatises, philosophical inquiries, and critical analyses meticulously crafted by Moulana Baqir Agah. From his penetrating insights into matters of faith and doctrine to his rigorous refutations of doctrinal misconceptions, each chapter offers a glimpse into the intellectual brilliance of a scholar ahead of his time.

Moulana Baqir Agah's scholarly journey is a testament to the transformative power of knowledge and the enduring legacy of intellectual inquiry. Rooted in the rich tradition of Islamic scholarship, his writings serve as a beacon of light, guiding seekers of truth towards a deeper understanding of the divine mysteries that shape our world.

As we embark on this journey of discovery, let us approach each chapter with humility and an open mind, for within the pages of this compendium lies the wisdom of generations past, waiting to be unearthed and embraced by all who seek enlightenment.

Moulana Baqir Agah (1158-1220) was born to Muhammad Murtaza, also known as Muhammad Saheb, the son of Md. Baqir of Bijapur. His father migrated to Vellore, where Moulana Baqir Agah was born on the 14th of Muharram in 1158 A.H. Initially, he studied under his paternal uncle Muhammad Habeebullah, who served Nawab Abdul Hye Khan. Later, he learned Persian and mysticism from Syed Shah Abul Hasan Qurbi of Vellore. He then moved to Natharnagar with his uncle Moulvi Habibullah, where he studied Arabic under Moulvi Waliullah. Encouraged by Waliullah, he pursued independent study, thoroughly examining significant works available to him. He composed poems in praise of his teacher Qurbi, impressing him with his talent. Returning to Vellore around 1179 A.H., he continued his studies under Syed Shah Abul Hasan Qurbi for several years. After Qurbi's death in 1182, Agah went to Madras and served Nawab Muhammad Ali Walajah as a tutor to his sons Nawab Umdatul Umara and Nawab Amirul Umara. He also corresponded in Arabic with Ghalib and Surur, the Shariffs of Mecca, and other Ulamas between 1185 and 1205 A.H. His reputation extended to scholars in North India due to his dispute with Moulana Ghulam Ali Azad Bilgrami (died in 1200 A.H.).

The contentious and derogatory comments made by Azad towards Agah were the primary reasons for the bitter dispute that lasted from 1196 to 1199 A.H. Agah recounts that during this time, Azad, likening himself to a crow nesting in the brain, and others like flies caught in a spider's web or mistakenly assuming they were hunting deer while they were mere flies, criticized certain expressions Agah had used. Agah responded with seven to eight written responses, objecting to Azad's critiques and annotating their verses for clarity. They engaged in debates over the interpretations and meanings of the verses. In 1199 A.H., Agah attributed the fault to Azad's words.

Azad himself grew weary of the controversy and attempted to reconcile with Agah in his old age, seeking solace in their past friendship, stating, "Oh, as an eighty-three-year-old, I wish for a few days the company of that kind and all acquaintances so that the dust of weariness does not settle on the edges of my mind and so that the remaining breaths come in a state of friendship. If not assisted, may God clear my mind of the world's ruin. Peace be upon you, and God's mercy and blessings."

In response, Agah acknowledged the real need for retribution, recounting how Azad scattered seven errors while Agah multiplied them to seven hundred in his writings, yet he restrained himself due to his patience, dignity, and willingness to forgive, limiting his response to four hundred errors and not adding unnecessary words to retaliate. He refrained from surpassing what was written and urged the importance of maintaining fairness and reflecting on past relationships, preserving the memories within the treasury of the heart. He emphasized the precious gem of friendship, which should not be discarded, and advised to keep the memory alive according to previous instructions.

He lamented Azad's passing in 1200 A.H. amidst their bitter feud, composing chronograms immediately upon hearing the news, expressing sorrow over the loss of such a distinguished individual. He mourned Azad's departure from the world and questioned the knowledge of the time.

Azad was freed from the shackles of tyranny, and I found myself bound by the chains of sorrow and regret. I sought solace for my soul, yearning for relief from the burden of his departure. With hindsight on the year of his passing, a hundred regrets echoed from the tip of my pen, each one a sigh of sorrow.

In 1204 A.H., at the invitation of Nawab Walajah, Moulana Abdul Ali Bahrul Uloom arrived in Madras from Bihar and was appointed as the principal of Madrasa-e-Kalan with a monthly salary of Rs.10,000, along with allowances.

The Shia-Sunni controversy erupted in 1207 and persisted until 1216 A.H. Baqir Agah authored about 54 treatises in Persian on various aspects of Imamat and Khilafat, which he later compiled into four volumes titled Kitab-al-Rasail fima yata'allaqu bil Imamati minal Masail in 1216. Agah himself provided a brief account of this contentious controversy, stating:

"He who had been fair-minded from the start, treating friends with tenderness and adversaries with courtesy, found himself entangled in the complexities of discord. He did not break anyone's spirit, but sought reconciliation. He never harbored bias in matters of faith, embracing both Sunni and Shia perspectives, engaging with both supporters and dissenters. He chose the path of peace and avoided conflict, especially during the reign of the late Nawab Amirul Umara Bahadur, who was a central figure in public affairs. He diligently worked to promote Shia interests within the region and sought support from other territories. Some had clear ties as disciples, while others sought only to correct poetic compositions, which was also a form of discipleship. During this period, none of them, nor any Sunni, heard bias in my discourse nor saw negligence in my work. If there was bias, it was countered with reason and respect, highlighting their strengths rather than their weaknesses."

"The late Nawab was impartial and supportive of the Sunni faith due to his influential status, bolstering their cause. Despite any inclination toward bias, he acted contrary to it and extended considerable support to these people. Envious individuals misconstrued this support as a pretext to malign their integrity, suggesting ulterior motives for their actions. After the passing of the late Nawab, these groups strayed from justice until the end of the reign of Nawab Walajah, may he be forgiven. They remained entrenched in their deceit, unwilling to emerge from the shadows of decorum and caution. As the late Nawab joined the ranks of the merciful, they resorted to deception and hypocrisy, masking their true intentions and projecting righteousness. They dug into the depths of ancient texts, twisting them with baseless accusations and unfounded suspicions against the esteemed figures of the caliphs, migrants, and supporters of truth. Their audacity led to utter devastation, distorting thoughts and manipulating sentiments with frivolous accusations, turning every instance of discourse into an opportunity for slander. One of them, whom I had shown kindness, borrowed a book from me, the

Quran, and kept it with him for a year. In his time of distress, he sent it to me from the port of Machilipatnam. After some time, upon perusing the book, I noticed three annotations. One of them pertained to a hadith, while another bore my name in abbreviated letters colored with the epithet 'infidel' inscribed upon the forehead of the Antichrist."

It may be written and pondered upon that all his audacity remained concealed, and no one pursued his malice. Another, who was a disciple and product of this individual, found himself disillusioned upon the transfer of Khawaja Rahmatullah Sahib, who had been his mentor, and was now found ensnared by the cunningly contrived scheme. The excerpt begins with:

"A man, a sheikh opposing Islam."

He was compelled to assert by virtue of authentic Hadiths, especially this one:

"The guidance of deeds which translates as follows: whenever bad innovations and slanderous accusations arise, my companions must manifest their knowledge during those times of turmoil. Anyone who fails to exhibit their knowledge during such times will be subject to the curse of Allah and the condemnation of angels and all creatures. This conduct, whether exhibited by the esteemed progeny or the companions of the honored Seal of the Prophets, peace be upon him, in the face of increasing weakness and illness, during the year 1207, was intended to repel the insinuations and doubts presented in the context of inheritance, devotion, and the written word."

"As soon as this treatise reached certain individuals, their countenances turned ashen, and the fire of turmoil and corruption, which had lain dormant in their hearts, ignited in the flames of discord. They stretched their tongues with futile words, weaving slanderous accusations and delusional ravings. They pained the aggrieved heart with their disgraceful insinuations, justifying it as a test: 'You will surely be tried in your possessions and yourselves, and you will surely hear from those who were given the Scripture before you and from those who associate others with Allah much abuse. But if you are patient and fear Allah, indeed, that is of the matters [worthy] of determination.'"

"The translation of this magnificent verse reads: 'Surely, We will test you with a bit of fear, hunger, and loss of wealth, lives, and crops. Give good news to those who patiently endure. When calamity befalls, they say, "Surely, we belong to Allah and to Him we shall return."' I penned this treatise, 'The Declaration of Exoneration,' when the fumes of chaos were at their peak. Afterward, I meticulously expounded upon the implications when faced with their brazen defiance, crafting the 'Treatise of Seeking Refuge in the One All-Powerful' upon hearing the braying of the donkey. Subsequently, they unleashed a barrage of assaults, reaching the zenith of their recklessness, culminating in the creation of numerous treatises, resembling the braying of a donkey, leaving each footstep mired in mud."

"Finally, they escalated into obstinacy and discord, resorting to attempts on my life annually during the month of Muharram, a period marked by fervent emotions. This sect of wickedness and deviation thrived on incitement, rebellion, and tumult. Each Muharram, they solemnized their pact of faithlessness, vowing to settle the matter this year, once and for all, by spilling so-and-so's blood. I witnessed the dwindling of these rebellions and endured the pangs of their afflictions, until my heart's anguish reached its climax, and the matter reached a boiling point. The verses of Khaqan Sharvani encapsulate the essence of this profound connection, leaving me bewildered and anxious."

"In the end, with great reluctance and a restless heart, on the last day of Dhu al-Hijjah, 1216 A.H., in the presence of Syed Arbab, the source of comfort and tranquility."

Spirit and reference of the people of revelation and conquest, the mirror-bearer of beauty, the remover of the veil of Muhammadan poverty, the unparalleled statue, the head of Ahmad's perfection, Hazrat Fatima, may the blessings and peace be upon her, the opening and closing prayers be upon her and her father, complete blessings and salutations be upon her forever. I have presented these quatrains alongside other quatrains and through the intercession of Hazrat Qudsiyyah, I sought the revelation of this dilemma and witnessed what I saw. Indeed, what has passed is past, mention it with goodwill and do not inquire about the news.

Agah has composed ten quatrains in praise of Hazrat Fatima, the last two of which are quoted below:

Those who are captive of desire and thoughts, consider me distant from you, O' Hazrat, I've entrusted this grievous tale to you, you know, and this assembly that slanderers conduct.

My heart is distressed by these baseless words, every moment, like the smoke of my heart, they scatter, and wrongly reward those who speak against me, if true, reward me.

This bitter controversy between the Sunnis and the Shias resulted in a serious conflict of opinion between Agah and Bahrul Uloom. The latter held the view that Muawiyah has only committed an ordinary mistake in opposing Ali and in raising arms against him. He cannot be treated as an unjust rebel.

Agah was of the view that Muawiyah was a rebel and he was not at all justified in raising arms against Ali. Agah quoted the following verses of Mulla Jami in support of his views:-

In opposition to another companion, that opposition he had with Haidar in war against him was an ugly mistake, the truth was in Haidar's hands, that opposition by the opponents is not commendable, but they shut their mouths against reproach and curse.

Agah refers here to the overthrow of Tajul Umara by the Britishers in 1216 A.H. = 1801 A.D. and the enthronement of Nawab Azimuddowlah, who was a Sunni by creed.

Bahrul Uloom argued that Jami has used the words of "ugly mistake" for the sake of maintaining rhyme. Agah got angry with him and has bitterly criticized him in a long poem, in which he says:

One of the scholars of India, who was famous in his time, protested with the words of "ugly mistake" in such a way that he portrayed Muawiyah as a diligent person who diligently sought the truth. Meaning, from the killers of Dhul-Nurayn, he sought compensation, not for kingdom or wealth, he waged war, his diligence led him to error, whoever engages in diligence, error is their sole reward, God granted him diligence like Ali's, his share of the right was twofold, grasp every error that arises from diligence, it was easy to convey a reproachful word, Maulana's verse is from the same rhyme, oh wise one, this is the essence of the speech of that virtuous one, after him, some ignorant people, misled by those distractions, may their harm not be a means to spreading confusion, connecting reason and religion, each one from that group, from the stupidity of reproach, made a jest, at Mulla Jami, who praised him despite his breath being faint, how could it be, if he doesn't retain breath by breath, it's not proper, the folly of ignorance, let those people write out, reflect on the heart, from the age of the three eras, select ones until the time of the righteous Imams, no one openly or secretly said, Muawiyah was diligent, rather they said he was all rebels, he trod the path of error, his rebellion became apparent, O' friend, after the killing of Ammar, the old sage of Jami said, war against him was an ugly mistake, the meaning of the mention is clear, surely, this ugliness has no limit, the limit of rejection.

Agah asserts that no objection has been raised against the use of such strong words like "خطا منکر" by anyone from Iran, Turan, and Hejaz, except Shaikh Ahmad Sarhindi and Bahrul Uloom, who have opposed the accepted views of Muslims across all countries and ages. He states: A learned man from Hind and a prominent figure from Khorasan have not expressed any objection to these words. Even in the face of this disagreement, no one from these esteemed territories has expressed dissent. Only after these distinguished personalities have spoken, has this issue been revived. This discourse lacks evidence and stands without proof. They have all traversed the path of error and wandered into the depths of misguidance, perhaps being influenced by false appearances. This criticism spans all eras, instigated by his adversaries' tongues, words laid bare without concealment.

Everyone acknowledged the truth about his conflict with Mirza Murtaza. It was beyond doubt a grave injustice and a serious offense. Whoever is acquainted with the news knows it to be true and widely known. Even if I were to record all these events, a separate book would be necessary for that purpose. If one were to adopt his stance, this statement would become null and void. It's quite astonishing that the eminent scholar who opposes Shaikh Ahmad has pursued this course of action. He blindly followed his lead, heedless of his advice. What he said, by framing "منکر" for the sake of rhyme, has made his speech remarkably strange. His articulation, if not careful, could reveal its limitations. Whichever way this statement is heard, it will emanate from the noble prince, prevailing in these times of trials, which saw a dearth of expansion and joy. The path of distress, traversed by friends, would otherwise not have led to the elevation of this discourse. Poets of the time recognized the greatness of Agah Jami and acknowledged his mastery without words. They all embraced his teachings, finding success and salvation through his melodious rhythm. In the realm of sacred poetry, where the stone of sanctity is employed in verses, one must not speak hastily without reflection. For in the superficial, one cannot find a solid foundation. Saadi, the wise, has expressed: "First, contemplate, then speak." This principle has laid the foundation for this verse. Thus, I have set forth this composition like a clear mirror. Finally, O observers, judge fairly. Whoever possesses a clear heart from God's grace, his method is always fair.

Agah authored works such as "Kamal-al-Insaf," "Ain-ul-Insaf," and "Ma'zitat Nama-e-Agahi," expressing disapproval of Bahrul Uloom's evasive stance during a critical juncture.

Agah passed away on the 14th of Zulhaj, 1220 A.H., and was laid to rest in the courtyard of his residence in Kishanpet, Madras.

He was the pioneer writer in South India to compile books on various topics in Hindi (Urdu). Proficient in Arabic, Persian, and Urdu, he mastered these languages and penned his works in Urdu for the benefit of those unable to comprehend Arabic and Persian. He authored over twelve works in Urdu alone, and also compiled a significant number of books in Arabic and Persian.

His Arabic works include:

1. "Tanwir-al-Baseerat-i-Wal Basar fis Salat-i-Al-an-Nabiyyi bi-Zik-al-Siyar," containing prayers praising the Prophet, along with an introduction discussing their significance and virtues.
2. "Maqamat-e-Weluriya Moulana," comprising five assemblies modeled after Hariri.
3. "Al-Nafhat-al-Anbariya fis salawt Ala Khair-al-Bariyya," featuring forty long poems praising the Prophet and Shaikh Abdul Qadir Jeelani.
4. "Tilka Asharatun Kamilatun Hindiyyah," containing ten long poems honoring the Prophet and other saints, mirroring the rhymes and meters of pre-Islamic Muallaqa writers.
5. "Diwan-e-Agah," presenting his lyrical poems in Arabic.
6. "Al-Dur-run-Nafees fi Sharh-i-Qawl-e-Muhammad bin Idris," a commentary on the statement of Muhammad bin Idris.
7. "Al-Qawl-ul-Mubeen fi Zarari-al-Mushrikeen," discussing the dangers of idolaters.
8. "Nafais-un-Nikat fi Irsalihi Alaihis-Salam ila Jamee il Mukawwanat," addressing the messages sent to all beings.
9. "Hawashi Ibn Kathir," comprising notes on Ibn Kathir's history.

He also composed a long Qasida in Persian titled "بحر اللطایف" about Abdul Qadir Jeelani, and concluded it with praise for Shah Abul Hasan Qurbi. Qurbi greatly appreciated this qaseedah. Later, Agah penned a commentary on this poem in Arabic.

He authored various works, including a prologue with thirteen sections, discussing the life and character of Hazrat Abdul Qadir Jeelani.

"Shamaim-al Shamail bi Nashr-i-Lataim-al-Rasail" is a collection of Arabic letters he penned between 1180 to 1205 A.H. to individuals like Shariff Surur, Shariff Ghalib, and others, representing Nawab Mohammed Ali Walajah, Nawab Amir-al-Umara, and himself to scholars and learned individuals of holy places.

In Persian, his works include:

Volume II :

1. "Tuhfat-al-Ahsan fi Manaqib-is-Sayyad Abil Hasan," a short work about Qurbi, divided into a preface and ten sections.
2. "Saadat-e-Sarmadiya fi Wujub-e-Muhabbat-e-Muhammadiya," written in 1202 A.H., emphasizes the importance of loving the Holy Prophet, divided into a preface, two chapters, and a conclusion.
3. "Chahar Sad Irad bar Kalam-i-Azad," a critical study of the flaws in Mir Ghulam Ali Azad's poetry in Arabic and Persian, written in 1199 A.H.
4. "Naghma-e-Bedil Nawaz," compiled in 1204-1205 A.H., also known as "Khursheed-e-Dil" and "Zahay Latifah-e-Ghaib Agahi."
5. "Kashf-al-Ghita an Ashrat-i-Yaum-al-Jaza," written in 1203 A.H., discussing the conditions preceding the Day of Resurrection.
6. "Sehr-ul-Halal fi Qasayid-al-Hilal," a collection of long poems praising the first moon by various poets, including his own contribution.

7. "Kitab-al-Rasail," consisting of 51 tracts dealing with Shia and Sunni controversies, divided into four volumes.

These works reflect his diverse interests and contributions to literature and scholarship in both Arabic and Persian languages.

Volume III:

- "Maqamaat al-Hadid fi Qim' Mat'ane al-Manhaj wa al-Tajreed," written in 1207 A.H.
- "Al-Barq al-Waamid al-Kashf Hufoat al-Rawafid," composed in 1214 A.H.
- "Kashf al-Istirar an Mushabihat al-Rawafid bi al-Kuffar," completed in 1209 H.
- "Al-Hujaj al-Nahidah fi Hukm al-Rafidah," authored in 1214 A.H.
- "Kamal al-Adl wa al-Insaf al-Dal 'Ala al-I'tisaf," completed in 1209 H.
- "Rad al-Kathib 'Ala al-Kathib al-Munkir bi Sharaf al-Mulqab bi al-Sahib," written in 1215 A.H.
- "Al-I'lan bi al-Adhan 'Ind Taghul al-Ghilan," penned in 1215 A.H.
- "Al-Isti'adha bi al-Wahid al-Qahhar 'Ind Samai Nahiqa al-Himar," written in 1215 A.H.
- "Tabyeen al-Insaf wa Tawheen al-I'tisaf fi Akhbar al-Shi'a min al-Khilaf," authored in 1215 A.H.
- "Al-Nuqool al-Badi'ah fi Aqsam al-Shi'a Raf' al-Tashajur 'An Hukm al-Tawatur," completed in 1215 A.H.

Vol. IV:

- "Sharh Rubaiyat Badi'ah dar Manaqib Shia," penned in an undisclosed year.
- "Tahriri ke ba Hadith Antum A'lam bi Amur Dunyakum Taluq Darad," written in an undisclosed year.
- "Ba'z Rawayat ke Yeki az Shia bazam Mawafiqash az Kutub Ma Baravarad," composed in an undisclosed year.
- "Tahriri ke ba Ba'z Rawayat Baravarad-e Shia Taluq Darad," authored in an undisclosed year.
- "Tahrir I'tifaqee ke ba Beit 'A- Zu al-Shahada Shud Laqab al-Kh Taluq Darad," written in an undisclosed year.
- "Rawayat Motazameenah Fazail Taqiyah wa Wajib Amal bar An az Kutub Ma'tabara Imamiyah Athna Ashariyah," composed in an undisclosed year.
- "Dala'il Athna Ashariyah dar Rad Ba'z Hufoat Imamiyah," written in an undisclosed year.
- "Tahriri ke ba Daw Bayt 'Aqaid Nama Hazrat Maulana Jami Quds Sirah Taluq Darad," authored in an undisclosed year.
- "Al-I'tisam bi Kalami al-Imam fi Mani' Lan Ahl al-Sham," written in an undisclosed year.

2. Kamal-i-Dana'i va Haq Namayi dar Bayan.

- Bad Paemai-i-Bahai

(Wind Measurement of the Bahai)

- Kamal-i-Rasani dar Bayan-i-Ighlat-i-Bahai

(Complete Exposition of Bahai Errors)

- Tawzih al-Bayan fi Tafzih al-Buhtan

(Explanation of Clarification in Exposing Falsehood)

3. Rad al-Buhtan al-Mawhum al-Muta'alliq bi Sayyidatina Ruqayyah wa Umm Kulthum

(Refutation of Alleged Falsehoods Associated with Our Lady Ruqayyah and Umm Kulthum)

6. Tanbih al-Salik bi Takdhib man Nasab al-Muta'ah ila al-Imam Malik

(Warning to the Seeker Against Falsely Attributing Pleasure to Imam Malik)

- Rad al-Fudul al-Muta'lliq bi Qawl Sahib Jami' al-Usul

(Refutation of Curiosity Related to the Statement of the Author of Jami' al-Usul)

- Mu'adhara Namah-i-Aghahi

(Letter of Apology and Awareness)

9. Kamal al-Insaf

(Perfection of Justice)

10. 'Ayn al-Insaf

(Source of Justice)

11. Is'af al-Muram fi Tahqiq al-Iman wa al-Islam

(Aid to the Will in Investigating Faith and Islam)

12. Ibarat-i-Raz-i-Naftah dar Sharh Ruba'iyat-i-Sitta

(Disclosure of the Hidden Secret in the Explanation of the Six Quatrains)

13. Ruba'iyat-i-Badi'ah dar Bayan-i-Mu'taqidat-i-Shi'ah az Ilahiyat va Nabuwwat va Imamat va Ma'adhiyat va Tafwihat-i-Inha bihaquq

(Excellent Quatrains in Exposition of Shiite Beliefs from Divinity, Prophethood, Imamate, and Resurrection and the Disproof of Their Falsehoods)

14. Rad al-Nisnas al-Mu'tarid 'ala Hadith al-Qirtas

(Refutation of the Objector to the Tradition of the Paper)

15. Nazm al-Faraid fi Sharh Ba'di Abiyat al-'Aqaid

(Verse of Benefits in Explaining Some Verses of Beliefs)

16. Daf' al-Shakk fi al-Fadk

(Removal of Doubt in the Reward)

17. Nur al-'Ayun fi Tafsir al-Sabiqun al-Awwalun

(Light of the Eyes in the Interpretation of the Ancient Ancients)

18. Idah al-Shams li Azahat al-Mutah

(Sunlight to Dispel Pleasure)

19. Sab'a Siyarah dar Rad-i-Mulhidan-i-Badkaran

(Seven Journeys in Refuting the Misguided Infidels)

20. Rad al-Had wa Fasad dar Mas'alah Rawayat Afa'al wa 'Ibad

(Refutation of Straying and Corruption in the Issue of Narrating Actions and Worship)

21. Nafat al-Musdur ila al-'Alim bi Zat al-Sudur

(Invitation to the Knowledgeable Regarding the Essence of the Hearts)

22. Al-Burhan al-Naqid li Asas Buhtan al-Rafidah

(The Evident Proof Against the Foundation of the Slander of the Shia)

23. Tuhfah-i-Har 'Aziz ba Tamiz dar Qissa-i-Ghulam va Kaniyz (Precious Gift with Distinction in the Tale of the Boy and the Maiden) Ahsan al-Tabyin fi Adab al-Muta'allimin (The Best Explanation of the Etiquette of the Students) (pp. 53 x 11). It is a book on the methods and purpose of teaching to the students and their duties and responsibilities towards their teachers and of the teachers towards the students. It is divided into four sections (فصول). Chapter five explains the etiquette of students concerning their teachers, divided into sixteen sections. The fourth chapter elaborates on the etiquette of students related to their studies and their predecessors, divided into forty-one subsections.

24. "Iqaz-al-Ghafileen" (Awakening of the Unaware) is compiled in 1185 A.H., addressing a literary dispute regarding the preference between a poet and a writer. A copy of it can be found in Kutub Khana-e-Sayeedia, Hyderabad.

25. "Kuhl-ul Jawahir fi Sharh Jila-il-Basair" consists of sixty-two sections and was written in 1185 A.H. It deals with the critique of arguments favoring poets over writers.

26. "Igaz-al-Niyam-lil-Itimam-i-bi Muqallid-i-Kulli-Imam" discusses whether adherents of one school of thought can follow another. It delves into the historical context of differing opinions and the complexities surrounding religious adherence.

These manuscripts address intricate religious and literary debates, challenging entrenched biases and advocating for nuanced understanding.

27. "Bayan-e-Dilnihed dar Sharh-i-Rubai Mustazad" is a commentary by Agah on the Rubaiyat composed by Mirza Abdul Qadir Bedil. It discusses the metaphorical elements within the verses and explores the depth of their meanings.

28. "Al-Manhal-al-Azb-al-Rawi fi Sharh-i-Muftatah al-Mathnawi" is a commentary on the initial verses of Moulana Rum's Mathnawi, compiled by Agah in 1208 A.H. In its introduction, he reflects on the complexity of interpreting these verses and the challenges of capturing their essence in writing.

This commentary, divided into two chapters, presents a comprehensive analysis of the text, addressing previously overlooked nuances and shedding light on its deeper philosophical and literary implications.

29. "Naqz-e-Iradha-e-Beja" is a rebuttal by Agah against criticisms leveled by certain Iranians against "Al-Manhal-al-Azb-al-Rawi." The year of compilation is discerned from a chronogram embedded within the text.

30. "Risala dar Radd-e-Mutariz ke bar Sharh-e-Bait-e-Mathnawi Shareef" is a response to objections raised against Agah's interpretations of the opening verses of the Mathnawi.

31. "Risala Tanbeeh al-Taeh fil Ghawayat il-Ghaeh bi Zanbiyat al-Jihad fi Martabat-il-Wilayah" is a commentary by Agah on select lines of the Mathnawi, drawing from the insights of Wali Muhammad. Manuscript copies of these works are preserved in the personal collection of the late Afzalul Ulama Dr. Abdul Haque at Kurnool. "Afghan-e-Nai dar Sharh-e-Ghazal Awwal

Hazrat Khwaja Hafiz" is a commentary on the first Ghazal of Hazrat Khwaja Hafiz by Agah. It delves into the nuances of the Ghazal and offers insights into its interpretation and significance.

32. "Diwan in Persian" is a collection of Persian poetry, with a manuscript copy held by Dr. Muhammad Ghouse, a descendant of Moulana Baqir Agah's paternal uncle Moulvi Habeebullah.

Conclusion:

As we draw the curtains on this journey through the life and legacy of Moulana Baqir Agah, let us pause to reflect on the profound impact of his scholarship and the enduring relevance of his teachings. In a world plagued by uncertainty and strife, his unwavering commitment to truth and intellectual inquiry serves as a guiding light, illuminating the path towards a more enlightened future.

May the insights gleaned from these pages inspire future generations to carry forth the mantle of intellectual curiosity and scholarly rigor, ever mindful of the transformative power of knowledge to shape our understanding of the world around us. And may the legacy of Moulana Baqir Agah continue to serve as a beacon of hope, guiding humanity towards a brighter and more enlightened tomorrow.

3. Moulana Abdul Ali Bahrul Uloom

In the pursuit of knowledge and enlightenment, the exploration of philosophical realms and metaphysical concepts has been a timeless endeavor of humanity. The works of Moulana Abdul Ali Bahrul Uloom stand as a testament to this enduring quest for understanding. Through his meticulous writings and scholarly insights, Moulana Bahrul Uloom delved into various aspects of Greek philosophy, metaphysics, scholasticism, and logic, enriching the intellectual landscape of his time and leaving a profound legacy for generations to come.

In this compilation, we embark on a journey through the vast corpus of Moulana Bahrul Uloom's works, meticulously curated and presented for the discerning reader. From his insightful commentaries on classical philosophical texts to his profound reflections on the nature of existence and mysticism, each work encapsulates the depth of Moulana Bahrul Uloom's intellectual prowess and his unwavering commitment to the pursuit of truth.

Through this compilation, it is our earnest endeavor to shed light on the remarkable contributions of Moulana Abdul Ali Bahrul Uloom, inviting readers to engage with his profound insights and timeless wisdom.

Introduction:

In the annals of intellectual history, few figures stand as tall as Moulana Abdul Ali Bahrul Uloom. Born into a lineage of scholars and thinkers, Moulana Bahrul Uloom emerged as a beacon of knowledge and enlightenment during a period marked by profound philosophical inquiry and scholarly discourse. From his early education under the tutelage of renowned scholars to his prolific writings and teachings, Moulana Bahrul Uloom's intellectual journey was characterized by a relentless pursuit of truth and understanding.

The works of Moulana Bahrul Uloom span a wide array of subjects, ranging from Greek philosophy and metaphysics to scholasticism and logic. Each work reflects his deep engagement with the philosophical traditions of both East and West, offering profound insights into the nature of existence, the mysteries of the cosmos, and the human quest for meaning.

As we delve into the pages of his writings, we are invited to embark on a journey of intellectual discovery-a journey that traverses the realms of thought and contemplation, seeking to unravel the mysteries of existence and illuminate the path to enlightenment.

Moulana Abdul Ali Bahrul Uloom (1144-1225 AH) was born into the family of Mulla Nizamuddin, the grandson of Mulla Qutbuddin who was martyred in Lucknow. His grandfather was killed in a local tribal conflict in Sihali on the 19th of Rajab, 1103 AH. The family migrated to Lucknow and settled in Farangi Mahal. Mulla Qutbuddin was renowned for his expertise in Greek philosophy, metaphysics, and logic, with several authored books.

Mulla Nizamuddin, Mulla Qutbuddin's third son, studied under scholars in Benares and Shamsabad before lecturing on philosophy until his death in 1161 AH. He contributed to various scholarly works. Mulla Abdul Ali received education from his father and Mulla Kamaluddin of Sihali. Due to sectarian disputes, he moved to Rohilkhand and later served in Rampur and Burdawan. Eventually, he was invited to Madras by Nawab Walajah, who appointed him Principal of Madrasa-e-Kalan. Nawab Umdatul Umara later honored him with the title Malikul Ulama and granted him a Jagir. Despite British interference, he remained steadfast in his principles.

He vehemently opposed British attempts to alter the ruling authority and continued teaching until his death in 1225 AH. He was buried in the Walajah Mosque compound in Madras.

Moulana Bahrul Uloom was deeply interested in Greek philosophy, metaphysics, scholasticism, and logic, and he authored numerous books on these subjects. Every day, he received continuous respect and honor from people for his contributions to the advancement of knowledge. Even after the passing of Nawab Umdatul Umara, the respect and honor for him continued, although the monthly stipend he received did not continue due to his lack of interest in worldly matters. His eminence and excellence were well-known from east to west, and his followers ensured the preservation of his high status and treated him with utmost respect.

Moulana Abdul Ali Muhammad, may peace be upon him, and his servants, were more deserving of maintaining their esteemed positions than the deceased Nawabs, given their devotion and service during his transfer. Therefore, it is hoped that the authorities would consider providing for the needs of Moulana Abdul Ali Muhammad's followers and servants, enabling them to devote themselves to worship and prayers for divine blessings and prosperity.

Here are some of his significant works:

1. "Fawatih-al-Rahmut" (630 pages x 27 lines), a commentary on "Musallam-al-Thubut" by Muhibbullah of Bihar, written in 1180 A.H.
2. "Sharh-e-Sullam-ul-Uloom" (210 pages x 15 lines), a commentary on the logic book by Mulla Muhibbullah of Bihar, written after completing his education.
3. "Rasail-al-Arkan" (288 pages x 27 lines), a book discussing the four fundamentals of Islam for students of Islamic Law and Jurisprudence.

4. "Tanvir-al-Manar," a Persian commentary on "Manar-al-Anwar" by Hafiz Abul Barakat Abdullah bin Ahmad Nasafi.
5. "Ahwal-e-Qiyamat" (184 pages x 19 lines), a book on the conditions and signs of the Day of Resurrection.
6. "Al-Hashiya al-as-Sadra," written on the Sharh Hidayat-al-Hikmah by Sadruddin Shirazi.
7. "Al-Hashiya ala Hashiya Mir Zahid," glosses on the glosses of Mir Zahid.
8. "Al-Hashiya ala Hashiya Mir Zahid ala Mulla Jalal," explanatory notes on Mir Zahid's glosses on Mulla Jalal's book.
9. "Taliqat-al-al-Ufaq-al-Mubeen": Mir Baqir Damad authored a book titled "al-Ufaq-al-Mubeen" on philosophy, and Bahrul Uloom provided explanatory notes on this commentary. Refer to Catalogue Rampur State Library No. 830 for details.
9. "Al-Ujalat-un-Nafia": This book, comprising 314 pages, covers various aspects of metaphysics. A manuscript copy of the book can be found in Rampur State Library No. 399.
10. "Al-Hashiya ala Hashiya Mir Zahid al-ar Risalat-al-Qutbiyyah": These are notes on Mir Zahid's commentary on the book by Qutbuddin Shirazi.
11. "Sharh-al-Zabita": A concise treatise of 44 pages, focusing on a specific aspect of logic. It was printed at Muhammadi Press, Madras in 1273 A.H.
12. "Sharh Mathnawi Moulana Rum": A Persian commentary on Mathnawi Moulana Rum, spanning three large volumes. It was

printed at Nawal Kishore Press, Lucknow. A meticulously transcribed copy by Hafiz Ahmad Khan Bahadur is available in the Library of Diwan Sahib Bagh, Madras.

13. "Wahdat-al-Wujud": In this brief tract, he delves into the contentious problem regarding the theory of Unity of Existence.

14. "Tanazzulat-i-Sitta": This tract discusses the question of the six stages of the personality of God, at the request of Nawab Muhammad Ali Walajah.

15. "Sharh-al-Fass-in-Nuhi": A commentary on a section of Fusoos-al-Hikam by Ibn-i-Arabi.

16. "Risalah-e-Sughra fis Suluk": A brief article on mysticism, about fourteen pages in length.

17. "Hidayat-al-Sarf": A short book on Arabic etymology in Persian, written for the benefit of his son Abul Ala. It was printed and published in Madras several times.

18. "Sharh-u-Asma-i-Ahl-il-Badr": Providing details about those who participated in the battle of Badr.

19. "Risalah fi Taqsim al Hadith": A copy of this work is available in Rampur State Library No. 126.

20. "Al-Hashiya al-al-Muthannat bit Takrar": A copy of this work is housed in the British Museum, London.

21. "Sharh Magamat al-Mabadi": (Located in Asifiya Library, Hyderabad No. 1314.)

Moulana Abdul Ali Bahrul Uloom had four sons and one daughter. Moulvi Abdul Rab, the third son, resided in Madras for an extended period and received stipends from the Nawab of Arcot. He passed away on the 26th of Ramadhan 1253 A.H., in Madras and was laid to rest in the compound of Walajah Mosque. The daughter was married to Mulla Alauddin Ahmad, who served as the Principal of Madrasa-e-Kalan of Madras and continued as a teacher until his demise on the 10th of Shawwal 1242 A.H. In 1218 A.H., he authored a commentary in Persian on Fusool-i-Akbari by Moulvi Ali Akbar Allahabadi, which was prescribed as a text on Arabic etymology in Arabic Madrasas.

Conclusion:

In the tapestry of intellectual history, the contributions of Moulana Abdul Ali Bahrul Uloom shine brightly as a beacon of enlightenment and wisdom. Through his insightful writings and profound reflections, Moulana Bahrul Uloom has left an indelible mark on the philosophical landscape of his time, inspiring generations of scholars and thinkers to ponder the mysteries of existence and strive for intellectual excellence. As we reflect on the rich tapestry of his works, we are reminded of the timeless relevance of his teachings and the enduring power of his ideas. In an age marked by uncertainty and upheaval, the writings of Moulana Bahrul Uloom serve as a guiding light, offering solace to the seeking soul and inspiration to the aspiring intellect.

May his legacy continue to inspire and enlighten future generations, guiding them on the path to truth, knowledge, and enlightenment.

4. Sharaful Mulk Bahadur

In compiling the following passages, we aim to shed light on the remarkable life and contributions of Sharaful Mulk Bahadur, a figure whose endeavors spanned disciplines from calligraphy to jurisprudence, leaving an indelible mark on his era. Through meticulous research and exploration, we delve into his prolific works, traversing realms of literature, theology, and scholarship. By chronicling his journey, we strive to honor his legacy and offer readers a glimpse into the multifaceted personality of a distinguished individual whose impact reverberates through history.

Introduction:

The life of Sharaful Mulk Bahadur unfolds as a tapestry woven with threads of intellectual pursuit and scholarly endeavor. Born into a milieu rich in academic tradition, he embarked on a journey marked by relentless pursuit of knowledge and excellence. From his early days studying Arabic and Persian under esteemed mentors to his later forays into metaphysics and mysticism, Sharaful Mulk Bahadur's thirst for understanding propelled him forward on a path adorned with scholarly achievements.

Through the annals of time, his name became synonymous with erudition and enlightenment. His literary oeuvre, spanning treatises on jurisprudence, theology, and linguistics, reflects a profound engagement with the intellectual currents of his era. As a calligraphist par excellence, he breathed life into the written word, infusing it with elegance and grace. His meticulous copies of sacred texts stand as testament to his mastery of the pen and the parchment.

In the following passages, we navigate the labyrinth of Sharaful Mulk Bahadur's life, tracing the contours of his intellectual landscape and unraveling the tapestry of his legacy. From the scholarly salons of Madras to the corridors of theological discourse, his presence looms large, casting a long shadow over the annals of history. Through meticulous research and thoughtful reflection, we endeavor to pay homage to a luminary whose brilliance continues to illuminate the corridors of knowledge.

Moulvi Muhammad Ghouse Sharaful Mulk Bahadur (1166-1238 A.H. 1752-1822 A.D.). He was the son of Moulvi Nasiruddin ناصر الدين Muhammad son of Qazi Nizamuddin Ahmad Sagheer, (the junior), was born at Arcot on 7th Ramadhan 1166 A.H.1752 A.D. He studied Arabic and Persian under his grandfather at Arcot and after his death in 1189 A.H. 1775 A.D., he was sent to Sivaganga, Ramnad to study metaphysics, scholasticism and philosophy under Moulvi Ameenuddin Ahmad Khan Bahadur, (d on 6th Ramadhan 1195 A.H. 1780 A.D.), who created in him a good taste for these sciences. After his death he began to take lessons on mysticism from Moulvi Waliullah of Natharnagar (Trichnopoly) (d 1205 A.H. = 1790 A.D.), who permitted him to the prayers, described in the book Dalail-al-Khairat دلائل الخيرات written by Imam Jazuli. He then came to Madras and was employed in the service of Nawab Amirul Umara (d 1203 A.H. 1788 A.D.); when Moulana Abdul Ali Bahrul Uloom came to Madras in 1204 A.H. 1789 A.D., he joined his class as a faithful student, and studied under him Greek philosophy, logic and scholasticism and at the same time copied the notes of this teacher on the commentary of Sadruddin Shirazi in 1206-1207 A.H. 1791-1792 A.D. He was then appointed a tutor to Nawab Azeemuddowlah. During the regime of Nawab Umdatul Umara he was not given any respectable post. Hence he took permission and after leaving his wife and children at Siddhout, he went over to Hyderabad in 1213 A.H.= 1798 A.D. He received the news of the sudden death of his wife at Siddhout on account of the snake bite, which made him more perturbed and puzzled and he was exhausted. He met Mir Alam, Mir Arastu Jah and the other dignitaries of Hyderabad state. But he was not given any post there also. He got disheartened and wrote a magama under the name of Zawajir-al-Irshad زواجر الارشاد, in Arabic, depicting the bad social and moral conditions of the the city of Hyderabad and its people. He did not waste his time there also. He copied the book of Shams-e-Bazigha شمس بازغه and then returned to Udayagiri, Nellore in A.H. Syed Abdul Qadir Khan, the Jagirdar of the place, granted him a monthly allowance and hence he lived there for about a year until he received a letter from Nawab Azeemuddowlah, inviting him to come to Madras and take charge of the post of Diwan, on a monthly allowance of Rs. 130/-. He was also awarded the title of Sharaful Mulk Bahadur. He took charge of this post from 9th Jamadiul Awwal 1216 A.H.=1801 A.D. He served the Nawab faithfully. But after seven years of service he tendered his resignation on 11th Ramadhan 1223 A.H. 1808 A.D., and spent the rest of his life in teaching and writing books. The students from all parts of the city of Madras gathered round him and he continued to teach them till he died on 11th Safar 1238 A.H., and was buried in the compound of the Big Mosque, Triplicane, Madras. He has written several works in Arabic and Perslan. The following are some of them. Works in Arabic. 1. Nathr-al-Marjan li Rasm-e-Nazm-al-Quran نثر المرجان فى رسم نظم القرآن. He began this lofty work at the instance of his beloved teacher Moulana Abdul All Bahrul Uloom and the encouragement of Abdul Ghaffar Khan Thabit Jung Bahadur (1189-1229 A.H. = 1775-1813 A.D.)

Moulvi Muhammad Ghouse Sharaful Mulk Bahadur (1166-1238 A.H. 1752-1822 A.D.) was born in Arcot on the 7th of Ramadhan in 1166 A.H. (1752 A.D.). He received his early education in Arabic and Persian under his grandfather in Arcot. After his grandfather's demise in 1189 A.H. (1775 A.D.), he pursued further studies in metaphysics, scholasticism, and philosophy in Sivaganga, Ramnad, under the guidance of Moulvi Ameenuddin Ahmad Khan Bahadur. Later, he delved into mysticism under Moulvi Waliullah of Natharnagar.

He later moved to Madras and served Nawab Amirul Umara. Subsequently, he joined Moulana Abdul Ali Bahrul Uloom's class to study Greek philosophy, logic, and scholasticism. He also served as a tutor to Nawab Azeemuddowlah. However, during Nawab Umdatul Umara's reign, he was not offered any respectable position, which led him to move to Hyderabad.

In Hyderabad, despite efforts to secure a position, he faced disappointment. He expressed his observations and frustrations through his work "Zawajir-al-Irshad," highlighting the social and moral issues of Hyderabad. After a brief stay in Udayagiri, Nellore, he received an invitation from Nawab Azeemuddowlah to return to Madras and serve as Diwan, which he accepted.

During his service as Diwan, he was titled Sharaful Mulk Bahadur. After seven years, he resigned and dedicated the remainder of his life to teaching and writing. He passed away on the 11th of Safar in 1238

A.H. (1822 A.D.) and was buried in the compound of the Big Mosque in Triplicane, Madras. His contributions include several works in Arabic and Persian, with "Nathr-al-Marjan li Rasm-e-Nazm-al-Quran" being one of them.

Works in Arabic:

1. "Nathr-al-Marjan li Rasm-e-Nazm-al-Quran" (نثر المرجان فی رسم نظم القرآن): He commenced this significant work under the guidance of his esteemed teacher Moulana Abdul All Bahrul Uloom and with the encouragement of Abdul Ghaffar Khan Thabit Jung Bahadur (1189-1229 A.H. = 1775-1813 A.D.). He completed the work in 1226 A.H. The text is structured into a muqaddima and two maqalas. In the muqaddima, he discusses the fundamentals of the art of Quranic script. The first maqala comprises five chapters () where he delves into the essential principles of the script. The muqaddima and the first maqala span 93 pages. The second maqala addresses the script of Quranic verses chapter by chapter. It was printed at Osmani Press and released under the auspices of Majlis-e-Ishaatul Uloom (مجلس اشاعت العلوم) in Hyderabad across several volumes.
2. "Al-Fawaid-al-Sibghiyya" (الفوائد الصبغيه): It is an Arabic commentary on the renowned poem "Al-Faraiz-al-Rahbia" (الفرايض الرحبيه) concerning inheritance. Written in 1232 A.H. (1816 A.D.), it was intended for the benefit of his sons Moulvi Abdul Wahab Madarul Umara Bahadur and Moulvi Muhammad Sibghatullah Qazı Badruddowlah Bahadur.

3. "Sawati-ul-Anwar fi Marifat-al-Awqat wal Ashar" (سواطع الانوار في معرفة الأوقات والاسحار): This brief Arabic work focuses on determining prayer and fasting times. It comprises a muqaddima and three babs. He also includes their Tamil equivalents under the subject of zodiacs. He penned this work in 1199 A.H. (1784 A.D.).
4. "Bast-al-Yadain II Ikram-al-Abawain" (بسط اليدين لاكرام الابوين): This work addresses proper behavior towards parents. It consists of a muqaddima, two sections (فصول), and khatin, written in 1205 A.H. (1790 A.D.).
5. "Kifayat-al-Mubtadi fi Figh-al-Shafai" (كفاية المبتدى في فقه الشافعي): A concise work of 36 pages on Shafai fiqh, composed by him in 1184 A.H. (1770 A.D.).
6. "Zawajir-al-Irshad Ila Ahl-e-Dar-il-Jihad" (زواجر الارشاد الى اهل دار الجهاد): A short treatise of 11 pages discussing the style of Hariri's magamat, depicting social and moral issues of Hyderabad and its people. His son Qazi Badruddowlah wrote a detailed commentary on this work.
7. "Taliqat ala Sharh Qatr al-Nada" (تعليقات على شرح قطر الندى): Notes on the well-known Arabic grammar text Qatr-al-Nada.
8. "Urjuzatun fi Alqab-e-Hazrat Ameerul Momineen Ali ibn Abi Talib" (ارجوزة في القاب حضرت امير المومنين على بن ابي طالب): Explanation of the names and titles of Hazrat Ali.
9. "Rasail-al-Barakat fi Sharh-i-Dalall-al-Khairat" (رسائل البركات في شرح دلايل الخيرات): A commentary on Dalail-al-Khairat, though left incomplete.

10. "Taliqat ala Mukhtasar Abi Shuja" (تعليقات على مختصر ابى شجاع): Notes on the figh book Mukhtasar Abi Shuja.

11. "Al-Najm-al-Waqqad fi Sharh-i-Qaseeda-e-Banat Suad" (نجم الوقاد في شرح قصيدة بانت سعاد): Explanation of Qaseeda-e-Banat Suad.

12. "Majmua-e-Masail-e-Figh Shafai" (مجموعة مسائل فقه شافعى).

13. "Rugat-i-Arabi" (رقعات عربى): Arabic letters written by him to various individuals.

14. "Nuhur-ul-Faraid-wa-Buhur-al-Faraiz" (نحور الفرائد وبحور الفرائض): A chart depicting the share allocation in family inheritances.

15. "Kafi Mukhtasar Kafiya" (كافى مختصر كافيه).

16. "Shafi Sharh Kafi".

17. "Juz-un-fi Salat al-Tasbeeh" (جزء في صلوة التسبيح).

18. "Hawashal-al-Qamus" (حواشى على القاموش): Annotations on Firuzabadi's Qamus dictionary.

The following works in Persian were authored by him:

19. "Anhar-al-Mafakhir" (انهار المفاخر): It narrates the life of Hazrat Shaikh Abdul Qadir Jeelani, divided into eleven rivers. Written in 1209 A.H. (1794 A.D.), it was printed at Haldari Press, Madras in 1297 A.H. (1879 A.D.).

20. "Basaim-al-Azhar fis Salat-i-ala Sayyid al-Abrar" (بسائم الازهار في الصلوة على سيد الابرار 125): Composed in 1204 A.H. (1789 A.D.) and printed at Mazharul Ajaib Press, Madras in 1270 A.H., it is divided into ten chapters.

21. "Al-Yawaqit-al-Manthura Azkar-il-Mathura" (اليواقيت المنثوره في الاذكار الماثوره): A translation of the Prophet's prayers into Persian,

completed in 1227 A.H.-1812 A.D., structured into a muqaddima, eight chapters (باب), and a khatima.

22. "Hidayat-al-Ghawi Al-al-Manhaj-al-Sawl fit Tibb-in-Nabawi" (هداية الغوى على المنهج السوى في الطب النبوى): A commentary on Suyuti's Al-Manhaj-al-Sawi on Greek medicine, likely initiated in 1189 A.H. (1775 A.D.).

23. "Rashhat-ul-Ijaz fi Tahqeeq-al-Haqeeqat wal Majaz" (رشحات الاعجاز في تحقيق الحقيقة والمجاز): A concise work on rhetoric spanning 30 pages, with examples drawn from the Quran, written in 1205 A.H.

24. "Khawas-sul-Haiwan" (خواص الحيوان): Originally his grandfather's notes on animal properties, edited by him in 1194 A.H.

25. "Burhan-al-Hikmah" (برهان الحكمه): A Persian translation of Hidayat-al-Hikmah in Arabic by Atheeruddin Mufazzal ibn Umar on metaphysics, divided into a muqaddima, four marsad, and a khatima.

26. "Khulasat-al-Bayan" (خلاصة البيان): A Persian commentary on Aqaid-e-Jami عقائد جامی written by Moulana Jami, completed by his son Moulvi Abdul Wahab Madar ul Umara Bahadur in 1269 A.H. (1852 A.D.).

27. "Risala dar Radd-e-Khwaja Kamaluddin Khan" (رساله در رد خواجه كمال الدين خان): Observations on the theological replies given by Khwaja Kamaluddin Khan.

28. "Fatawa-e-Nasiriya" (فتاوی ناصريه): A collection of judicial decrees issued by his father Moulvi Nasiruddin Muhammad but edited by him.

28. Fatawa-e-Nasiriya is a compilation of judicial decrees issued by Moulvi Nasiruddin Muhammad, edited by his son. It begins with an Arabic introduction justifying the four schools of Muslim Law: Hanafi, Maliki, Shafi'i, and Hanbali.

29. "Amadan" is a concise treatise discussing the root words of Persian and their conjugations.

30. "Zubdat-al-Aqaid" is a brief treatise outlining the principles of faith.

31. "Siham-al Naqira fi Uyun-al-Nazira" is likely a small book covering the principles of debate and discussion.

Sharaful Mulk Bahadur was skilled in calligraphy and copied numerous works, as detailed in "Khanwada-e-Qazi Badruddowlah." In 1226, he prepared an embroidered copy of the Holy Quran with notes by Hafiz Tahir bin Arab bin Ibrahim al-Isphahani, a student of Imam Muhammad bin Muhammad bin al-Jazri.

Sharaful Mulk Bahadur also had a keen interest in Greek medicine, mathematics, and astronomy, evident in his books on these subjects, showcasing his remarkable talents and intelligence.

He married Haleema Bee, daughter of Hafiz Muhammad Sayeed, with whom he had four daughters and three sons. After Haleema Bee's death in Siddhout on 30th Rabi I 1213 A.H. (1796 A.D.), he married Aisha, daughter of his uncle Moulvi Ghulam Abdul Qadir, with whom he had no children. Two daughters and a son died young. His sons, Moulvi

Abdul Madarul Umara and Moulvi Muhammad Sibghatullah Qazi Badruddowlah, gained prominence as administrators and authors, as discussed in Chapter IV. His daughters were married to Syed Qasim Nawaz Khan Bahadur and Moulvi Safiuddin Muhammad Nasir, as previously mentioned.

Conclusion:

As we draw the curtains on our exploration of Sharaful Mulk Bahadur's life and works, we are left with a profound sense of awe and admiration for the indomitable spirit of scholarship that defined his existence. His unwavering commitment to the pursuit of truth and enlightenment serves as a beacon of inspiration for generations to come.

In traversing the terrain of his achievements, we have encountered a polymath whose contributions transcend the boundaries of time and space. From his scholarly treatises to his artistic endeavors, Sharaful Mulk Bahadur's legacy endures as a testament to the enduring power of knowledge and creativity.

As we bid farewell to this journey of discovery, let us carry forth the torch of learning ignited by Sharaful Mulk Bahadur, honoring his memory and perpetuating his legacy for posterity. May his life serve as a guiding light for all those who seek to unravel the mysteries of the universe and enrich the tapestry of human civilization with the threads of wisdom and insight.

Bibliography

Al-Attas, S. M. N. (1993). Islam and secularism. Kuala Lumpur: ISTAC.

Al-Dimasyqi, A.-I. A.-N. (2016). Syarh Shahih Muslim. Dar al-Kutub al-`Ilmiyah.

Allen, C. (2013). Islamophobia. In Islamophobia. https://doi.org/10.4324/9781315745077-41

al-Maraghi, M. (2002). Tafsir al-Maraghi. Beirut: Darul Fikir.

Al-Qaradawi, Y. (2010). Islam an introduction. Kuala Lumpur: Islamic Book Trust.

al-Qurtubi, A. A. M. ibn A. (2014). Tafsir al-Qurtubi (Vol. 20). Beirut: Dar al-Kutub al-'Ilmiyah.

Al-Qushayri, I. (2018). Tafsir al-Qushayri. Dar Ihya' al-Turath al-Arabi.

Al-Rāzī, F. (2000). Al-Tafsīr al-Kabīr aw Mafātih al-Gayb, Vol. VII. Dar Al-Hadith.

Al-Sya'rawi, A.-I. A.-M. (2007). Tafsir Al-Sya'rawi. Qitha' al-Saqafah wa al-Kutub.

Al-Syawkani, M. bin A. (2014). Fath al-Qadir al-Jami' baina Fannai al-Riwayah wa al-Dirayah min 'Ilm al-Tafsir, Vol. 5. Dar Ibnu Hazim.

Al-Thabathaba'i. (1987). Tafsir Al-Mizan. Islamic Publications Office.

Al-Zuhaily, W. (2009). Al-Tafsir al-Munir fi al-Aqidah wa al-Syariah wa al-Manhaj. Dar al-Fikr.

APS (Applied Social Psychology). (2017). The Role of Religion in Prejudice Enablement and Reduction. Retrieved December 26, 2022, from https://sites.psu.edu/aspsy/2017/09/28/the-role-of-religion-in-prejudice-enablement-and-reduction/

Bakhshi Hazrat 'Alī Aḥmed and Rizwānur Raḥmān. (2012). Glimpses of the Holy Qur'ān. (New Delhi: Adam Publishers and Distributors).

Chelini-Pont, B. (2013). Relationship between Stereotyping and the Place of Religion in the Public Sphere. In J. Svartvik,

Jesper & Wiren (Ed.), Religious Stereotyping and Interreligious Relations (pp. 75–84). Palgrave Macmillan.

Geertz, C. (1977). The Interpretation of Cultures. Basic Books.

Geertz, C. (2013). Religion as a cultural system. In Anthropological Approaches to the Study of Religion (pp. 1–46). https://doi.org/10.4324/9781315017570

Hanafi, H. (2000). Islam in the modern world: Religion, ideology and development vol. I. Cairo: Dar Kabaa.

Hanafi, H. (2006). Culture and civilizations, conflict or dialogue? Vol. I the meridian thought. Cairo: Book Center for Publishing.

Jafari, F. (2020). Theological knowledge in Islamic mysticism and gnosticism." Kanz Philosophia A Journal for Islamic Philosophy and Mysticism 6(2). DOI: https://doi.org/10.20871/kpjipm.v6i2.92.

Karama, M. J., & Khater, N. A. (2020). Educational peace theory in the holy qur'an. Al-Bayān – Journal of Qur'ān and Ḥadīth Studies, 18, 138–154.

http://scholar.ppu.edu/bitstream/handle/123456789/2214/1.pdf?sequence=1&isAllowed=y

Khairulnizam, M., & Saili, S. (2009). Inter-faith dialogue: The qur'anic and prophetic perspective. Journal of Usuluddin, 9(2), 65–94.

Khaldun, I. (2015). Muqaddimah. Cairo: Dar-Ibnu al-Aitam.

Kidwai, Salim. (1996). Hindustani Mufassirein Awr Unki' Arabi Tafsirein (in Urdu) .(New Delhi:Maktaba Jamiah).

Kokan, Moḥammad Yousuf. (1960). Arabic and Persian in Carnatic, (Madras: Hafiza House).

Ma'roof M M M. (1995). *Spoken Tamil dialect of the Muslims of Sri Lanka: Language as Identity classifier*. Islamic Studies 34 (4).

Nashir, H. (2015). Understanding the ideology of Muhammadiyah. Muhammadiyah University Press.

Nieuwkerk, K. van, LeVine, M., & Stokes, M. (2016). Islam and popular culture. University of Texas Press.

Patji, A. R. (1991). The Arabs of Surabaya: a study of sociocultural integration. Canberra: Australian National University.

Putra, A. D., Purnomo, D., & Utomo, A. W. (2019). Sociological study of harmony in diversity: Lessons from Salatiga. Walisongo: Jurnal Penelitian Sosial Keagamaan, 27(1), 69–98. 10.21580/ws.27.1.3504

Ridwan, M., & Robikah, S. (2019). Ethical vision of the qur'an: Interpreting concept of the qur'anic sociology in developing religious harmony. Jurnal Ilmiah Islam Futura, 18(2), 308–326. http://dx.doi.org/10.22373/jiif.v19i2.5444

Sanaa Sha'lan, 'Adore Me'(A'shaquni), Daira al-Maktaba al- Wataniyya, Hashemite Kingdom of Jordan, Third Edition, 2016.

Saerozi, M. (2017). Dynamics of the development of istiqomah mosque in front of a church in Ungaran Central Java Indonesia. Journal of Indonesian Islam, 11(02), 423–458. 10.15642/JIIS.2017.11.2.423-458

Saged, A. A. (2021). Honoring the human self with a world peace study in the light of purposes the holy quran. Quranika: Journal of Libahuts Qur'an, 19(2), 223–234.

Shareef, Moḥammed Muṣṭafa and Bad'iuddin Ṣabri. (2008). Development of Tafseer Literature in India, (Hyderabad: Osmania University).

Shihab, M. Q. (2004). Tafsir al-mishbah. Jakarta: Lentera Hati.

Shu'aib, Tayka. (1993). Arabic, Arwi and Persian in Sarandib and Tamil Nadu, (Chennai: Imaamul Aroos Trust).

Thabari, I. J. (1999). Tafsir al Thabari. Kairo: Dar al Fikr.

Zamakhsyari, M. I. U. al. (2012). Al-kassyaf 'an haqaiq al-tanzil wa 'uyun al-ta'wil fi wujuh al-ta'wil. Cairo: Dar al-Hadis.

Zubair, K M A Aḥamed. (2010). *Tamil-Arabic Relationship*, ed. John Samuel G, (Chennai:The Institute of Asian Studies Press).

Zubair, K M A Ahamed. (2012). *Eminent Scholars of Sheik Sadaqathullah Appa's Family and their contribution to*

Arabic and Islamic Studies, (in Arabic), Thaqafatul ḥind 54, (3&4).

Zubair, K M A Ahamed. (2013). *Qasaid al-Madaih al-Nabaviyya fi Tamil Nadu,* (in Arabic), Thaqafatul ḥind 64, (4).

Zubair, K M A Aḥamed. (2017). Prophet's Panegyrics in Arabic Literature, (Moldova: Lambert Academic Publishing).

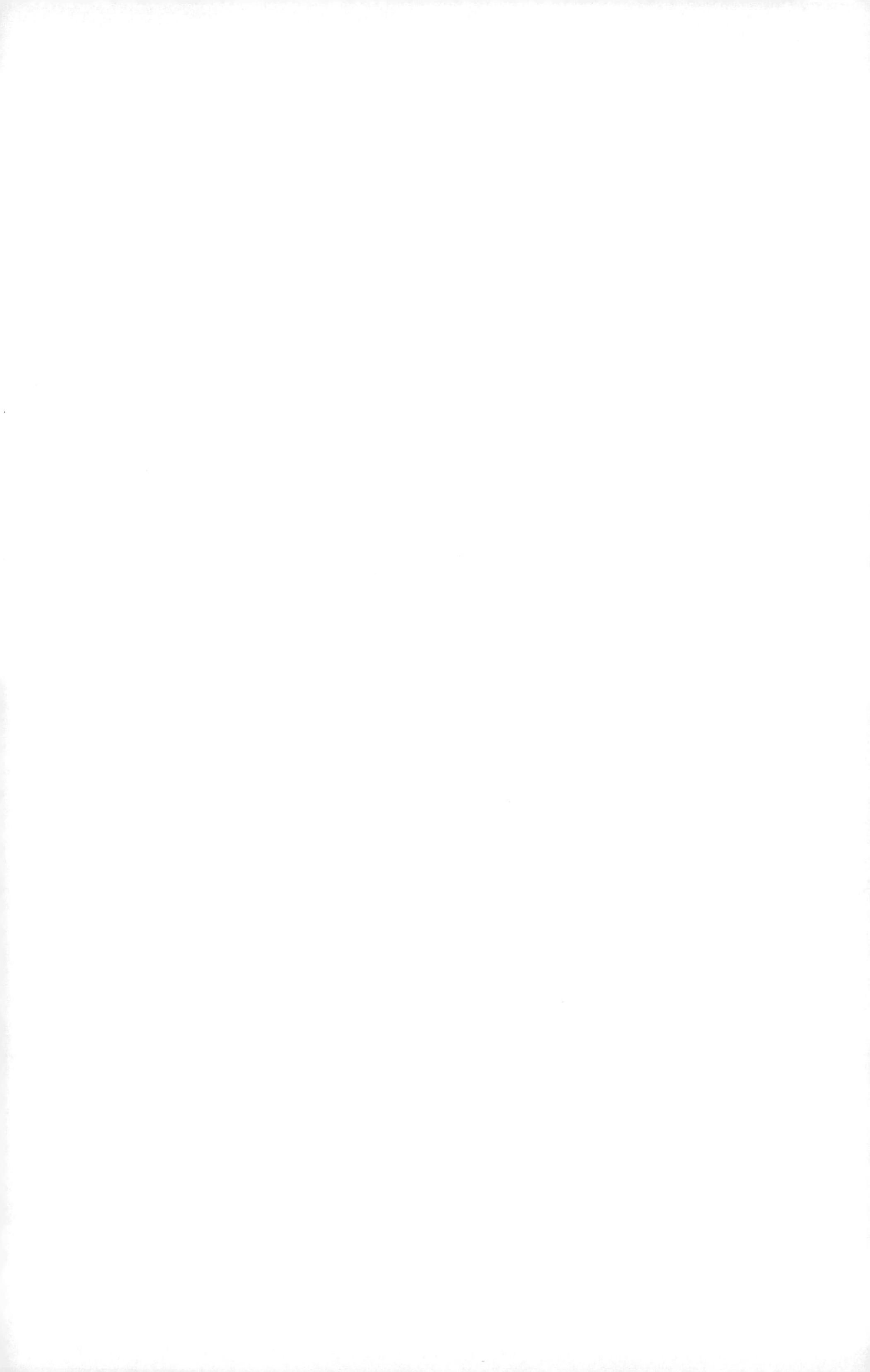

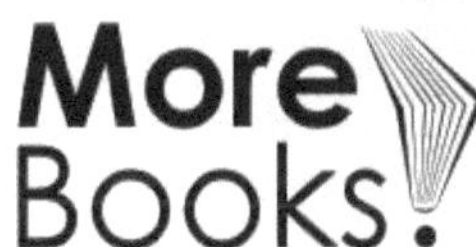

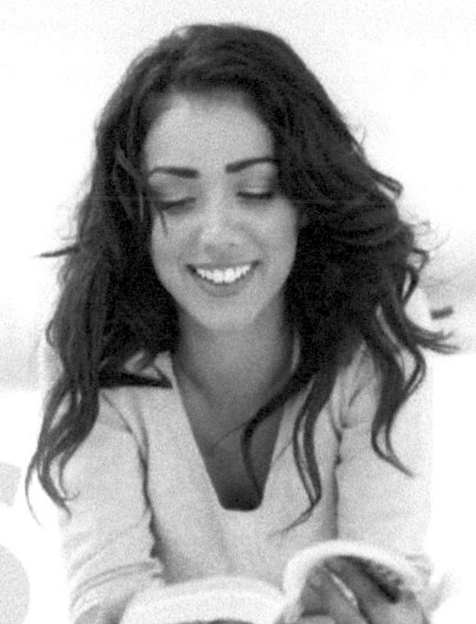

yes

I want morebooks!

Buy your books fast and straightforward online - at one of world's fastest growing online book stores! Environmentally sound due to Print-on-Demand technologies.

Buy your books online at

www.morebooks.shop

Kaufen Sie Ihre Bücher schnell und unkompliziert online – auf einer der am schnellsten wachsenden Buchhandelsplattformen weltweit! Dank Print-On-Demand umwelt- und ressourcenschonend produzi ert.

Bücher schneller online kaufen

www.morebooks.shop

info@omniscriptum.com
www.omniscriptum.com

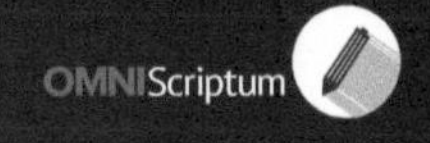

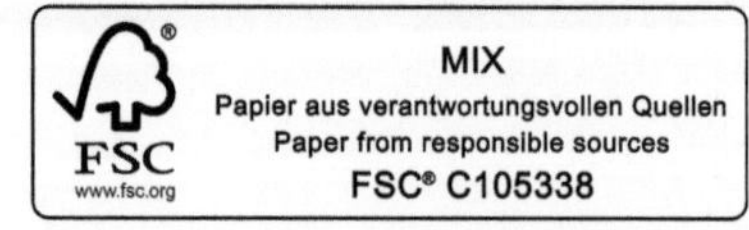

Printed by Books on Demand GmbH, Norderstedt / Germany